MAY 2010

W9-BDB-525

WITHDRAWN

Spectacular Animal Towns

The Bat's Cave
A Dark City

by Joyce Markovics

Consultants:

Susi von Oettingen, Endangered Species Biologist
U.S. Fish and Wildlife Service

Jim Kennedy, Conservation Biologist
Cave and Mine Resources Specialist, Bat Conservation International

BEARPORT
PUBLISHING

New York, New York

Des Plaines Public Library
1501 Ellinwood Street
Des Plaines, IL 60016

Credits

Cover and Title Page, © Michael Durham/Minden Pictures; TOC, © Craig Dingle/Shutterstock; 4, © Stephen Krasemann/Photo Researchers, Inc.; 5, © Merlin D. Tuttle, Bat Conservation International,www.batcon.org; 6, © Merlin D. Tuttle, Bat Conservation International,www.batcon.org; 7T, © Merlin D. Tuttle, Bat Conservation International,www.batcon.org; 7B, © Merlin D. Tuttle, Bat Conservation International,www.batcon.org; 9, © Merlin D. Tuttle, Bat Conservation International,www.batcon.org; 10, © Daniel Heuclin/NHPA/Photoshot; 11, © Stephen Dalton/Animals Animals Enterprises; 12, © Merlin D. Tuttle, Bat Conservation International,www.batcon.org; 13, © Merlin D. Tuttle, Bat Conservation International,www.batcon.org; 14, © Merlin D. Tuttle, Bat Conservation International,www.batcon.org; 15, Courtesy of Archivo Pronatura Noreste; 16L, © Kevin Schafer/The Image Bank/Getty Images; 16R, © Merlin D. Tuttle, Bat Conservation International,www.batcon.org; 17, © Nick Baker/ecologyasia.com; 18, © Joe McDonald/Visuals Unlimited/Getty Images; 19, © Merlin D. Tuttle, Bat Conservation International,www.batcon.org; 20, © Michael Fogden/Animals Animals Enterprises; 21, © Jim Clare/npl/Minden Pictures; 22, © Merlin D. Tuttle, Bat Conservation International,www.batcon.org; 23, © AP Images/Jake Schoellkopf; 24, © SuperStock, Inc./SuperStock; 25, © Joe McDonald/Corbis; 26, © Merlin D. Tuttle, Bat Conservation International,www.batcon.org; 27, © Mark Kiser, Bat Conservation International,www.batcon.org; 28L, © Rick & Nora Bowers/Alamy; 28C, © Michael & Patricia Fogden/Corbis; 28R, © David M Dennis/Oxford Scientific/Photolibrary 29T, © James Urbach/SuperStock; 29B, © Premaphotos/Alamy; 32, © Alexei Zaycev/iStockphoto.

Publisher: Kenn Goin
Senior Editor: Lisa Wiseman
Creative Director: Spencer Brinker
Design: Dawn Beard Creative
Photo Researcher: Picture Perfect Professionals, LLC

Library of Congress Cataloging-in-Publication Data

Markovics, Joyce L.
 The bat's cave : a dark city / by Joyce Markovics.
  p. cm. — (Spectacular animal towns)
 Includes bibliographical references and index.
 ISBN-13: 978-1-59716-871-7 (library binding)
 ISBN-10: 1-59716-871-8 (library binding)
 1. Bats—Juvenile literature. I. Title.

QL737.C5M362 2010
599.4—dc22

                    2009008146

Copyright © 2010 Bearport Publishing Company, Inc. All rights reserved. No part of this publication may be reproduced in whole or in part, stored in a retrieval system, or transmitted in any form or by any means, electronic, mechanical, photocopying, recording, or otherwise, without written permission from the publisher.

For more information, write to Bearport Publishing Company, Inc., 101 Fifth Avenue, Suite 6R, New York, New York 10003. Printed in the United States of America in North Mankato, Minnesota.

022010
010810CG

10 9 8 7 6 5 4 3 2

Contents

Bat Rush Hour

Just before the sun sets in South Central Texas, the summer sky comes alive. It's the time when Mexican free-tailed bats exit their home in Bracken Bat **Cave**. "For more than two hours they leave the cave and spiral higher and higher into the air," says **biologist** Gary F. McCracken.

A stream of Mexican free-tailed bats leaving Bracken Bat Cave

Bracken Bat Cave, located outside of San Antonio, Texas, houses the largest known bat **colony** in the world. There are more bats living in the cave than there are people living in Mumbai, India—one of the world's largest human cities.

At first, only a few bats fly out of the cave's dark opening. Then hundreds and thousands more swirl out. Soon a huge cloud of as many as 20 million bats has formed in the dark sky. The flapping bat wings make a whooshing sound. Finally, the Mexican free-tailed bats fly out of sight.

A Mexican free-tailed bat

A Supersize Cave

Bracken Bat Cave is huge—large enough to house the 20 million bats that **roost** there. Its entrance, a big hole in the ground, leads to a dark underground city. Unlike a human city that has many buildings, the cave is just one giant room, nearly 100 feet (30 m) wide.

Due to its large size, Bracken Bat Cave is the perfect home for millions of Mexican free-tailed bats. This type of bat has been living there for more than 10,000 years.

Mexican free-tailed bats also live in **abandoned** mines, tunnels, and under bridges.

During the day, the Mexican free-tailed bats rest and sleep safely in this giant city. They hang upside-down from the cave's jagged ceiling. Hooked claws and special **tendons** in their feet let them cling to the stony ceiling without tiring. In this position, they can hide from **predators** such as snakes or quickly launch into flight when it's time to feed.

Mexican free-tailed bats
roosting in Bracken Bat Cave

Inside Bracken
Bat Cave

On a Mission

The group that leaves Bracken Bat Cave each night is so large that it can be tracked by **radar**. Radar is commonly used to predict weather by following moving objects, such as raindrops, in the sky. "To the radar, the millions of bats emerging from their cave look like a huge storm," says Gary F. McCracken. Where are all these bats going?

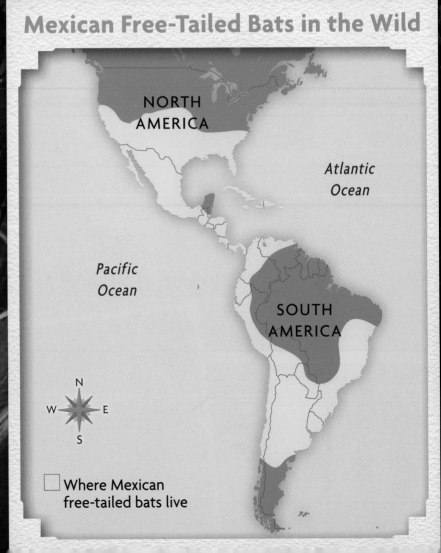

Mexican Free-Tailed Bats in the Wild

NORTH AMERICA

Atlantic Ocean

Pacific Ocean

SOUTH AMERICA

free-tailed
mostly in
ern United
d parts of
erica, which
Mexico, Central
South America,
slands of the
ies.

N
W E
S

☐ Where Mexican free-tailed bats live

Gary has learned that the bats leave Bracken Bat Cave to hunt insects in the surrounding area. How does he know this? The radar can also detect the billions of bugs that swarm the Texas sky.

The bats will eat about 200 tons (181 metric tons) of these bugs in one night. The insects, mostly moths and beetles, can destroy crops, so many farmers are glad to have the bats around.

This Mexican free-tailed bat has just caught a moth.

Some Mexican free-tailed bats can fly up to 250 miles (402 km) in a single night!

Winged Hunters

How do bats catch insects? As they soar high into the air, the bats use their wings to scoop **prey** into their mouths. All bats have almost hairless wings, which are like hands but with webbing to connect their fingers.

The world's largest bat is the giant golden-crowned flying fox, a rare fruit bat. It has a wingspan of five to six feet (1.5 to 1.8 m)!

Mexican free-tailed bats can fly up to 10,000 feet (3,048 m) high. They can also fly up to 60 miles per hour (97 kph)—as fast as a car on a highway!

Since it's dark when they hunt, bats use **echolocation** to find their prey. In this process, bats send out high-pitched sounds that travel in waves. These sound waves bounce off objects and return to the bats as echoes. Bats can determine the size and shape of an object and how far away it is by listening to the echoes.

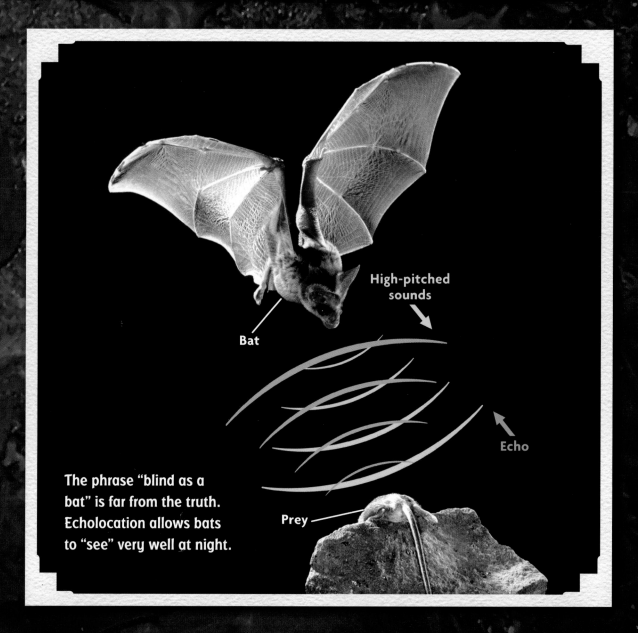

High-pitched sounds

Bat

Echo

The phrase "blind as a bat" is far from the truth. Echolocation allows bats to "see" very well at night.

Prey

Bat Nursery

After filling up on insects, the Mexican free-tailed bats return to Bracken Bat Cave. It is now time to feed their hungry babies, called pups. Millions of pups huddle together at the top of the cave, waiting for their mothers.

Mexican free-tailed bat pups

Each mother bat must be able to find her baby. How is she able to pick out the right one? A pup has a special call and scent. The pup starts calling for its mother as soon as it hears the adults fly into the cave.

Once a mother and pup find each other, the pup uses special teeth to latch on to its mom. Pups feed on their mothers' milk several times each day.

A Mexican free-tailed mother bat rests with her newborn baby.

mother bat

pup

Most of the bats living in Bracken Bat Cave are females and pups. Although some males live there, too, most live in nearby caves.

A Long Journey

Mexican free-tailed bats don't spend the entire year in Bracken Bat Cave. During the winter, they live in caves in Mexico to escape the cold Texas weather and to find enough food to survive. While in Mexico, male and female bats **mate**.

Cueva La Boca, a cave in Mexico, is one of the Mexican free-tailed bats' winter homes.

After winter ends, the bats **migrate** up to 1,000 miles (1,609 km) from Mexico to Bracken Bat Cave. The bats are back in Texas by March and the females give birth by June. This is a good time for the mothers to raise their pups as there is plenty of food in the area during the warmer summer months.

Bats leaving Cueva La Boca

Mexican free-tailed mother bats weigh between .4 to .5 ounces (11 to 14 g). A pup weighs about .1 ounce (2.8 g)— almost one-fourth of its mother's weight. That's one big baby!

Bat Homes

The Mexican free-tailed bat is just one of over 1,100 bat **species** in the world. Each species has a special home. Some bats roost in empty buildings or storm drains. Others find more unusual places. For example, Honduran white bats take shelter in the leaves of rain forest plants. They cut the leaves with their teeth in such a way that the leaves collapse into upside-down "tents." These little homes protect the bats from rain.

A close-up of a Honduran white bat

Honduran white bats make their home in a leaf tent.

In Southeast Asia, tiny club-footed bats roost inside bamboo stalks. To reach their home, the bats can squeeze into an opening as small as .4 inches (1 cm)—about the width of a fingernail.

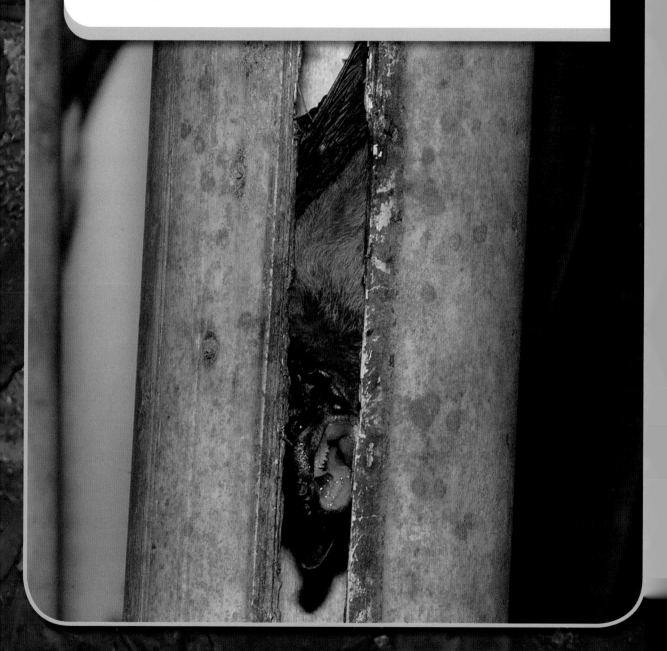

This club-footed bat rests in its bamboo stalk home. These bats, like most bat species, are active at night and rest during the day.

In West Africa, small woolly bats live in large spiderwebs!

Deep Sleep

During winter months, some bats **hibernate** in their homes rather than migrate to warmer **climates**. For example, little brown bats hibernate in caves when it is cold outside and food is **scarce**. Before winter, they eat as much as they can. This builds up fat, which stores energy and allows them to go without food for many months.

Little brown bats hibernating during winter

Little brown bats of North America can hibernate for up to six months.

During hibernation, little brown bats enter a deep sleep. To save energy, their body temperature drops, and their breathing and heartbeat slow. It is important to never disturb hibernating bats. Waking these animals may cause them to burn up the energy they need to survive the long winter.

A Special Diet

Bats that live in warmer climates don't need to hibernate because they can find food year-round. Vampire bats, for example, live in the warm climates of Latin America, where there is plenty of food. Groups of up to 1,000 vampire bats live in caves, empty buildings, or hollow trees. At night, they awaken in search of their favorite food—blood!

Vampire bats usually feed on the blood of sleeping **mammals**, such as cattle. First, they quietly walk toward their prey on all fours. Then they bite the animals on the legs or backs with their two front teeth. The bite is fast and painless. The victims are not seriously hurt and may even stay asleep during the attack!

A vampire bat lapping up the blood of a sleeping cow

Vampire bats do not actually "suck" blood. Instead, they lap up the blood with their tongues.

Vampire Behavior

Cattle are not the only animals that vampire bats hunt. Some white-winged vampire bats feed on chickens. These clever bats snuggle up to hens and pretend to be chicks. Once in position under the hens, the bats feed on their blood.

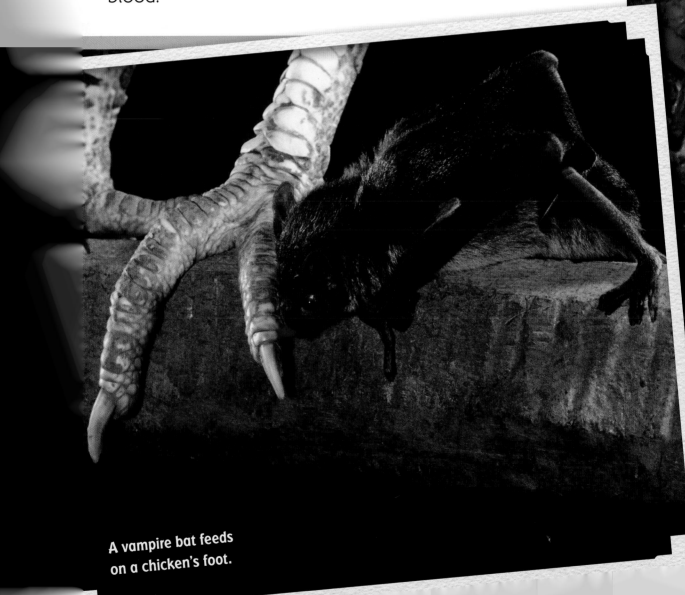

A vampire bat feeds on a chicken's foot.

Unlike other bat species, vampire bats work together to make sure all the bats in their colony get fed. Sometimes, vampire bats are not able to find food. Without a meal, these bats could starve to death in just a few days. Luckily, well-fed bats return to the cave and share their food by spitting up blood for hungry members of the colony.

A vampire pup

Vampire bat pups drink their mothers' milk for up to ten months. They are fed some blood when they are about two months old.

Then and Now

For thousands of years, vampire bats and other bat species have been feared and killed by humans. Why? People thought they would bite and spread disease. Though some bats do carry diseases, such as **rabies**, most do not.

While it's not a good idea for people to keep bats as pets or let them live in their homes, bats are not always dangerous. They usually only bite in self-defense or to get food.

Comic books portrayed bats as evil.

Today, there are people who still view bats as pests. They hunt these animals and destroy their homes. Some people close up the entrances to caves. Others knock down old buildings and seal off mines where the bats live. These animals now have fewer and fewer places to call home.

Bats live in the ceiling of this old church in Pennsylvania.

Wild bats should never be disturbed or handled. Bats that allow humans

The Future

Protecting bat **habitats** is a good way to help keep these animals safe. Some bat **conservation** groups have built special gates at cave openings. The gates prevent people from disturbing sleeping bats. In 1991, a group called Bat Conservation International (BCI) bought 692 acres (280 hectares) of land around Bracken Bat Cave to protect the bats and their habitat from people.

Scientists are building a gate at the entrance of Hubbard's Cave in Tennessee to protect bats.

More than half of all bat species in the United States are **endangered** or in decline. One of the reasons for the decrease in the bat **population** is habitat destruction. Another big reason is a mysterious illness called white nose **syndrome**. Little brown bats as well as other types of bats have been dying off in huge numbers from this sickness. The cause of the problem is not fully understood by scientists.

Another way to help bats is for people to build bat houses. These homes not only give the bats a safe place to live, but many farmers now put these up to attract bats because they eat the insects that can destroy their crops. More bats mean that there will be fewer insects to destroy human food. Scientists are hoping these efforts will keep bats safe and help their dark cities thrive for years to come.

opening

A bat house

Bat Facts

Many kinds of bats are social animals that live together in colonies. Here are some more facts about bats and their amazing colonies.

	Mexican Free-Tailed Bat	Vampire Bat	Little Brown Bat
Size	3.5 inches (9 cm) long	3.5 inches (9 cm) long	3 to 3.5 inches (8 to 9 cm) long
Wingspan	7 inches (18 cm)	7 inches (18 cm)	6 to 8 inches (15 to 20 cm)
Color	dark gray	usually dark brown, gray-brown, or reddish brown	brown
Food	moths, beetles, leafhoppers, and other insects	the blood of cattle, horses, chickens, and other animals	moths, beetles, mosquitoes, and other insects
Colony Size	up to 20 million	up to 1,000	up to 300,000
Life Span	about 11 years in the wild	about 9 years in the wild	20 to 30 years in the wild
Habitat	southern United States and Latin America	Latin America	North America

More Animal Towns

Bats are not the only animals that live in spectacular towns. Here are two others.

Weaver Birds -

- Weaver birds live in Africa in nests that hang from trees.
- Male weaver birds make the nests with grass stems and other plant parts.
- The nest looks like an upside-down bottle that has a tubelike entrance at the bottom.
- Many species of weaver birds are very social. They build their nests next to one another. There are usually several nests on one tree branch.

Social Spiders -

- Social spiders live in colonies in the rain forests of South America.
- They build giant hammock-shaped webs that hang from plants.
- The spiders' bodies are about the size of pencil erasers. The colonies can include up to tens of thousands of spiders.
- All the spiders act like one big family, guarding eggs against predators and feeding hatchlings.
- As a group, the spiders can capture prey ten times their size!

Glossary

abandoned (uh-BAN-duhnd) empty; no longer used

biologist (bye-OL-uh-jist) a scientist who studies plants or animals

cave (KAYV) an underground hole, often used by animals for shelter

climates (KLYE-mits) typical weather patterns in various places

colony (KOL-uh-nee) a group of animals sharing a home

conservation (*kon*-sur-VAY-shuhn) the protection of wildlife and nature

echolocation (*ek*-oh-loh-KAY-shuhn) the production and use of sound waves to find objects

endangered (en-DAYN-jurd) being in danger of dying out

habitats (HAB-uh-tats) places where plants or animals live

hibernate (HYE-bur-*nayt*) to enter a deep sleep during winter

mammals (MAM-uhlz) warm-blooded animals that have a backbone, have hair or fur on their skin, and drink their mothers' milk as babies

mate (MAYT) to come together to produce offspring

migrate (MYE-grayt) to go from one area to another at a certain time of year

population (*pop*-yuh-LAY-shuhn) the total number of a kind of animal living in a place

predators (PRED-uh-turz) animals that hunt other animals for food

prey (PRAY) animals that are hunted and eaten by other animals

rabies (RAY-beez) a deadly disease caused by a virus that attacks the brain and spinal cord and is spread by the bite of an infected animal

radar (RAY-dar) a system that uses radio waves to find moving objects in the sky

roost (ROOST) to settle or sleep

scarce (SKAIRSS) hard to find

species (SPEE-sheez) groups that animals are divided into, according to similar characteristics; members of the same species can have offspring together

syndrome (SIN-drohm) a group of signs or symptoms that are characteristic of a disease

tendons (TEN-duhnz) strong cords that join muscles to bones

Bibliography

Schutt, Bill. "The Curious Bloody Lives of Vampire Bats." *Natural History* (November 2008).

Tuttle, Merlin D. *America's Neighborhood Bats.* Austin: University of Texas Press (2005).

ngm.nationalgeographic.com/ngm/0204/feature7/index.html

www.batcon.org

www.nhm.ac.uk/nature-online/life/mammals/bats/session1/index.html

Read More

Editors of Time for Kids. *Time for Kids: Bats!* New York: HarperCollins (2005).

Lockwood, Sophie. *Bats.* Mankato, MN: The Child's World (2008).

Vogel, Julia. *Bats.* Minnetonka, MN: NorthWord Books for Young Readers (2007).

Williams, Kim, Rob Mies, Donald Stokes, and Lillian Stokes. *Stokes Beginner's Guide to Bats.* Boston: Little, Brown & Company (2002).

Learn More Online

To learn more about bats, visit
www.bearportpublishing.com/SpectacularAnimalTowns

Index

About the Author

Joyce L. Markovics is an editor, writer, and orchid collector. She lives with her husband, Adam, and their pet aquatic frog. She owes special thanks to Reuben Richardson, her guide to Anguilla's bat caves.